Contents

1 'City of the Mountains'

Monterrey is the third-largest city in Mexico and has a population of 2.9 million. It is one of the country's richest cities. Monterrey is in the northern state of Nuevo Leon, 215 km south of the US border. It is known as the 'City of the Mountains' because of the dramatic landscape that surrounds it.

Monterrey produces more than 75 per cent of Mexico's iron and steel, which were originally used in buildings, bridges and railways. Today they are used to make cars, electrical goods, aeroplane parts and much more. Monterrey's iron and steel industries have brought in a lot of money and the city is now a major centre for business. There are plenty of office jobs, in banks and insurance companies, for example. Many food and drink companies, particularly breweries, have also set up in Monterrey. The city has excellent schools and one of the best universities in the country.

Above all, it is the new *maquiladora* industries that are making the city rich today. These industries make brand-name goods, such as Levi jeans, which are then sold in other countries. Because Monterrey is close to the US border, it is ideally placed for companies, usually American or Japanese, who want to export their goods to the USA. The number of factories has grown from 81 to 224 between 1991 and 2000.

The growth in population and industry has had some negative results. Monterrey is heavily polluted and has a serious water shortage. The problem is so severe that the breweries have to bring water in by truck from 50 km away.

▼ *Monterrey's stylish modern business centre (bottom) displays a smelting pot (top) originally used in the city's iron industry.*

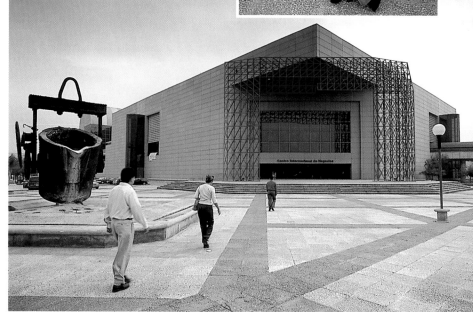

▲ *This map shows Mexico's main states, cities and landscape features.*

MEXICO: KEY FACTS

Area: 1,973,000 sq km

Population: 99.58 million (2000 estimate)

Population density: 50.5 persons per sq km (2000 estimate)

Capital city: Mexico City (16.4 million)

Other main cities: Guadalajara (3.3 million), Monterrey (2.9 million)

Highest mountain: Pico de Orizaba (5,610 m)

Longest river: Rio Bravo (Rio Grande) 2,100 km in Mexico (3,925 km in total)

Main language: Spanish

Major religion: Christianity (Catholicism)

Currency: Peso

2 Past Times

Some of the world's most impressive ancient civilizations existed in Mexico, from 1200 BC until the Spanish invaded in 1519. These civilizations included the Olmecs, the Mayas, the Zapotecs and the Aztecs. Mexico's ancient history is still clear today. The ruins of many great cities and pyramids remain in central and southern Mexico. They are popular tourist attractions and bring in millions of dollars.

The Spanish ruled Mexico for 300 years from 1519. They set up plantations to grow maize, cotton, sugar, vanilla and indigo. The crops were grown in Mexico and then taken by ship to Europe, where they could be sold for high prices. The cotton and sugar plantations remain important to Mexican farming today.

▲ Benito Juárez was a Zapotec Indian who became president in 1858. He set up a new government that tried to be fair to all the people in Mexico.

◀ The spectacular Pyramid of the Sun at Teotihuacán. This is one of the many reminders of the great civilizations that flourished in Mexico before the arrival of the Spanish in 1519.

Recent developments

The Partido Revolucionario Institucional (PRI) ruled
Mexico from 1929-2000, when it lost the elections. The
PRI is intended to represent the views of all the people.
But Mexico's unique system of government has become
terribly corrupt. A few people have become incredibly
rich while the poor have struggled to survive. Poverty
is still a very serious problem. In the state of Chiapas,
violent protests have often led to bloodshed.

The USA is one of the most important influences
upon Mexico today. Multinational companies
are setting up factories in the cities along the
US border at a fast rate. It is cheaper to make
goods in Mexico because workers are paid
less than in the USA.

▶ *Mexico's history has often been violent.*
The uprising in Chiapas has continued
into the twenty-first century.

IN THEIR OWN WORDS

'I am Miguela Marina. I am a Tarahumara Indian, and I live close to
the town of San Augustin in the west of Chihuahua State. Every
two months I travel to Chihuahua City to sell baskets and other
tourist objects in the main square. Life for my people has changed
drastically in recent years. Before, we would hunt deer by running
after them until they were tired enough for us to catch them.
Today we make baskets and mats from the leaves of the plants
that grow at the bottom of Barranca del Cobre (Copper Canyon)
to sell to tourists.'

3 Landscape and Climate

Mexico is the fourteenth-largest country in the world. It has an area of nearly 2 million square km and a wide variety of landscapes and climates.

Mountain ranges and the central plateau

The Western and Eastern Sierra Madre mountain ranges run roughly parallel to the coasts. There is also a rugged range of volcanic mountains in central Mexico. It includes the active volcano Popocatepetl (5,452 m) and, close by, Mexico's highest mountain, Pico de Orizaba (5,610 m).

The central plateau is about half of the total area of Mexico. Its southern half is, on average, over 2,000 m above sea level. It has several large lakes because it is surrounded by mountains, which stop the water from flowing to the sea.

Peninsulas

Mexico has two large peninsulas, Baja California and the Yucatán. Baja California is long, narrow and mountainous. It runs south from the US border for about 1,200 km.

▲ *This sacred* cenote *at Chichen Itza is typical of the sinkholes found in the Yucatán landscape.*

▼ *The volcano Popocatepetl, near Puebla, has frequent minor eruptions. In January 2001 it erupted five times.*

The Yucatán Peninsula is flat and juts out into the Gulf of Mexico. It has few rivers and no large lakes because the limestone bedrock is porous, allowing water to seep into it. However, huge rivers flow underground and *cenotes* (sinkholes), which look like gigantic wells, have formed where the roofs of underground river caverns have collapsed.

▲ *The northern coast of the Gulf of Mexico, with its warm sea and sandy beaches, has become a popular destination for holidaymakers.*

Deserts and coastal plains

North-western Mexico is mainly desert or semi-desert and has broad coastal plains. On the northern coast of the Gulf of Mexico, there are wide beaches, sand bars and swamps. The southern coastal plains are covered in lush vegetation.

IN THEIR OWN WORDS

'My name is Alejandra Reyes and I live in Saltillo, the capital of Coahuila State. I am a biologist and it is my job to monitor the unique wetlands at Quatrocienigas, which are right in the centre of the Chihuahua Desert. No one knows exactly why the pools have formed, but they are clearly connected to one of the underground rivers that flows beneath the desert. The grazing of too many horses and cattle is damaging the edges of the pools and churning up the mud. This is threatening the survival of rare fish species that breed in the shallow water at the edges of the pools.'

Changing climate

Mexico has a wide variety of climates, from the summit of Pico de Orizaba, where the temperature never rises above 0 °C to the heat of the Yucatán where temperatures can reach 34 °C. Most people live in the southern half of the central plateau. Here the average temperature is 17 °C and rainfall is as high as 1,000 mm each year, which is ideal for agriculture.

Baja California is Mexico's driest state, receiving only 0-300 mm of rain each year. The north of Mexico is getting drier and the deserts are expanding.

▲ More than half of Mexico is desert. These spectacular dunes are near Juárez in the increasingly hot and arid Chihuahua Desert.

◀ The summit of Pico de Orizaba is the coldest place in Mexico.

These changes are caused partly by global warming, and partly by the continuing destruction of Mexico's forests. The forests used to soak up the winter rainfall and release moisture throughout the year.

At the other end of the scale, the states of Chiapas, Veracruz and Tabasco are the wettest in Mexico, receiving 1,000-4,000 mm of rain each year.

The south-west of the country is being hit by hurricanes more often as global weather patterns change. Over the next ten years, the states of Guerrero, Chiapas and Oaxaca are expecting devastation from hurricanes even more often.

▲ *Mexico has extensive tropical rainforests in the south where rainfall is high.*

IN THEIR OWN WORDS

'I am Armando Hernandez. I am a taxi driver and I live in Chihuahua City. I moved here with my parents when I was 5 years old. That was more than 40 years ago, and there have been many changes to the landscape and climate around the city since then. In my childhood the place where I am standing used to be a large cattle ranch outside the city. The grass and the cattle have gone now and the area is desert.

'It is November and we have had no rain at all this year, which is very unusual. Even when it does rain, the water runs off the land directly into the rivers. The land cannot soak up water well because it has been damaged by forest clearance and over-grazing.'

Natural Resources

Oil has been Mexico's single most important export for over 50 years. It is the world's fifth largest oil producer, and has an average output of 334 million barrels a day. In 1999 the country had oil reserves of 58.2 billion barrels and is expected to remain a major producer for many years to come.

Minerals and non-minerals

Mexico is rich in deposits of precious metals, including gold and silver. It is the world's largest producer of silver, but many mines are closing because of the drastic drop in the world price for silver. Metals that are used in industry, including iron, copper, zinc and lead, are plentiful. There are also reserves of rarer metals such as antimony, arsenic, bismuth and mercury.

Only 5 per cent of Mexico has been properly explored for minerals. Mining will not be increased unless world prices go up dramatically.

Mexico is also rich in non-minerals and is the world's main producer of fluorite, celestite and sodium sulphate, and a major producer of graphite, barite and sulphur. These raw materials have a wide range of uses. Graphite, for instance, is used in pencil leads, and sulphur is used to make rubber more elastic.

Fishing

Mexico is not a major fishing nation, but it has over 10,000 km of coastline, which give it access to some very productive areas of the sea. Prawns are the most valuable catch for the fishermen. Mexico made US $672 million from fish exports in 1999, and most of this was from prawns. Mexico's fish stocks are under threat from pollution and from global warming, which is changing the sea temperature.

▲ The Minatitlán oil refinery in Tabasco distils crude oil to produce diesel, petroleum and other fuel products. Tabasco has Mexico's largest oil deposits, with vast offshore reserves.

▲ *Prawns are a favourite with the Americans. These Giant Pacific prawns can fetch as much as $1 each.*

IN THEIR OWN WORDS

'My name is Juan Xichlocan. I am one of only a few hundred Seri Indians who continue to live on the desert coast of the Gulf of California. We are fishermen by tradition and our main catch is crabs. We catch them by placing a crab pot on the seabed and leaving it there overnight. The price we get for our crabs has more than doubled in the last two years. Now it is easier for us to earn enough money to survive. The crabmeat is being sold as far away as Tokyo and New York. It is particularly valuable in the USA. The US crab stocks on the Atlantic coast have been over-fished and there are no longer enough to meet demand.'

Energy sources

Half of Mexico's power stations use oil to produce electricity. Another third, mainly in the south, are powered by hydroelectricity. Mexico also has geothermal, natural gas and nuclear power stations. Energy resources are so abundant that the country is able to export electricity and gas to the USA. The north uses oil and gas to generate electricity because most of its rivers are not big enough to power hydroelectric plants. There are plans to develop geothermal and solar sources of power in this part of the country.

Forests

While Mexico's natural forests are constantly decreasing, plantation forests are being expanded. These forests are grown to make money out of their timber. They have a smaller variety of trees in them than in the natural forests and do not provide the same habitat for wildlife. At the beginning of the twentieth century, firewood was collected by the many people who lived in the countryside. In the twenty-first century the demand is for fax paper, packaging and building materials.

Apart from timber, renewable resources, such as chicle latex, which is used in chewing gum, are also harvested.

▼ *Mexico is rapidly exhausting its natural forest resources. These planks of wood will be used in the building industry.*

Water

Northern Mexico receives very little rain and is heavily dependent on underground reservoirs for its water. But these supplies are being over-exploited and there are already serious water shortages.

In contrast, there is plenty of water in the southern states of Chiapas, Tabasco and Veracruz. These areas receive as much as 4,000 mm of rainfall each year.

▲ *Mexico has abundant water resources in the south but farmland needs to be irrigated in the north. This water is being pumped to cropland in the Chihuahua Desert.*

IN THEIR OWN WORDS

'My name is Eduardo Ramírez. I am a forest manager on the *ejido* (see pages 19 and 40) of Novek, which is a community-owned area near the city of Chetumal, Quintana Roo. Life here has improved enormously since we gained control of our land and forests twenty years ago. Before, a logging company employed a few people on very low wages and the rest of the community were subsistence farmers. Today, we manage our own forest, we have our own sawmill, and we have a bulldozer for maintaining the roads.

'There are plenty of jobs for people in the village and the standard of living is much higher. Before we only had a primary school, but today we have both primary and secondary schools and a new medical post. Many of our young people go to college in Chetumal to study forest management and then return to work on the *ejido*.'

5 The Changing Environment

The expansion of the deserts is one of the most serious environmental problems facing Mexico. In the last 50 years the massive desert areas in northern Mexico have been increasing in size, and they are still growing today.

The desertification of northern Mexico has a number of causes. The deserts were once surrounded by forests that regulated the local climate. They acted like a giant sponge, absorbing the rainfall and releasing water throughout the year. Because so much of the forests have been cut down, the fringes of the desert have dried up, and the arid area has grown. Trees are still cut down in the desert states of Chihuahua and Zacatecas, which provide 30 per cent of Mexico's timber. On top of this, millions of litres of water are extracted every day from the region's few major rivers. The water is used by farmers and people in the cities. Cattle and horses are allowed to overgraze and global warming is making the problem even worse.

▼ Serious overgrazing by horses and cattle has destroyed the natural vegetation in this part of the Chihuahua Desert.

Rainforests

The Mexican rainforests stretch into the Yucatán, Quintana Roo and Chiapas. They are part of *El Peten* – Central America's largest continuous area of rainforest, which stretches into Guatemala and Belize. The rainforests in the far south of Mexico contain jaguars, quetzals, hummingbirds and many other rare species. But over 25,500 square km of Mexico's rainforest were destroyed every year from 1990 to 2000, often to make way for coffee plantations and cattle ranches.

Some conservation projects have been started and 8 per cent of the rainforest is now protected. Forest management schemes are run by local communities that need to earn a living from the forest without destroying it.

▲ *Chicle collection is now managed under community schemes aimed at protecting the rainforest.*

IN THEIR OWN WORDS

'My name is Juan Carlos Bararra and I am an environmentalist and a marine biologist. The supply of water is a major problem throughout the entire north of Mexico. I am standing on the bottom of what should be the water reservoir for the city of Hermosillo. The city has a population of over 600,000. At present it has to get all of its water from deep bore holes. The underground water reserves are being used up much faster than they are being replaced. In twenty years' time the situation could be extremely serious. Changes in the local climate are adding to the water problem here in Sonora State. The rains are no longer reliable. Deforestation in the mountains and overgrazing in the desert are making the situation worse.'

Temperate and tropical dry forests

Mexico also has huge areas of temperate and tropical dry forest, made up mainly of oak and pine trees. The largest and least-touched forest is in Chimulapas, Oaxaca. These forests have been exploited for thirty centuries, intensively during the last two. Seventy per cent of the original forest has disappeared. Some excellent conservation projects have been set up to stop the destruction. But 99 per cent of Mexico's temperate and tropical dry forests remain unprotected.

Farming in the desert

Northern Mexico suffers from regular droughts. This makes irrigation essential for farming. Increasingly vast amounts of water are being channelled into the croplands. This is changing the flow of the region's major rivers. The balance of the desert habitat is endangered by the continued exploitation of its precious water supplies.

▲ This monarch butterfly reserve in Michoacán State is a protected area of the forest.

◄ Intensive farming of chilli plants under plastic in an irrigated field in Baja California. In 1979, 20.3 per cent of the cropland in northern Mexico was irrigated. By 1996, this had risen to 23.5 per cent.

Ejidos

Over 60 per cent of central and southern Mexico is divided into agricultural communities called *ejidos*. People on *ejidos* do not have proper ownership rights and are often very poor. Over-grazing by their animals is destroying the natural vegetation. The soil is also becoming exhausted, which affects the harvests. But this situation is changing. Since 1992, people have been allowed to sell or rent their land. Small holdings can now be combined into larger areas more suited to modern farming methods.

▲ *These children are campaigning about environmental issues. Children living on* ejidos *are taught about looking after the environment.*

IN THEIR OWN WORDS

'My name is Hugo Gayton Rodríguez and I live in the Chihuahua Desert with my family. We have a small farm but I make most of my money collecting a small plant called candelilla, which grows wild in the desert. I boil the plant stems with acid to produce wax. The wax is exported for use in car paints, lipsticks and polishes.

'But too much candelilla has been picked and the plants are becoming rare. Candelilla is difficult to grow. It is already extinct in some areas of the desert. If I cannot find a better way of harvesting the plant, I may be forced to move my family to one of the big cities to look for work.'

◀ *Pollution from the port of Guaymas on the Gulf of California threatens the natural habitat of whales.*

Urbanization

Nearly 75 million Mexicans now live in urban areas, which is causing major environmental problems. Air pollution has sharply increased over the last ten years. Between 1980 and 1995 carbon dioxide emissions increased by over 40 per cent, from 255 million tonnes per year to 357 million tonnes. Most of this is the result of heavier traffic – the number of cars in Mexico doubled between 1980 and 1996. Smog hangs over most of the country's major cities, including the northern cities of Juárez, Chihuahua, and Monterrey.

Mexico City is one of the most polluted in the world. It sits in a cloud of pollutants for the majority of the year. The smog includes carbon monoxide and lead. Lead poisoning is thought to cause brain damage. It is most

▼ *Twelve thousand tonnes of pollutants are added every day to the smog that hangs over Mexico City.*

worrying in children, whose brains are still developing. People in Mexico City have more than twice as much lead in their blood as people who live in the world's other major cities.

Various schemes have been set up to reduce the city's pollution. Public transport is cheap and efficient. The number of days on which cars can use the roads is restricted. But so far these schemes have made little difference to air pollution.

Water pollution is also a major problem for Mexico's cities. The Panuco River, for example, receives 690,000 tonnes of untreated sewage every year. The city of Juárez uses the Rio Grande as both its main water supply and its main sewer! Every day over 175,000 kg of organic waste are dumped in Mexico's rivers. Over half comes from the food and drinks industry. Other polluters include the metal, paper and chemical industries.

▶ *It is estimated that 75 per cent of Mexico's air pollution is caused by traffic fumes.*

IN THEIR OWN WORDS

'My name is Iliana Lopez Guerrera. I am 18 years old and I work at a bottled-drinks factory in Monterrey. I hope to move away soon because the pollution here is terrible – it is much worse than when I was a child. On some days the smog is so thick that you can't see the mountains that surround the city.

'I suffer from asthma and on really bad days I find it hard to breathe. I look forward to the rain because it cleans the air. Afterwards I can breathe easily and see the mountains again.'

6 The Changing Population

The Mexican population has two main origins. The first group are the Mexican Indians, who lived in Mexico before the Europeans arrived. The second group are the Europeans, who came to Mexico in 1519. Today, 75 per cent of Mexicans are *mestizo*, which means that they have a mixed ancestry, part Mexican Indian, part European. Another 10 per cent of the population are Mexican Indian. The remaining 15 per cent are African, Japanese and people from other Spanish-speaking countries.

At the beginning of the sixteenth century, around 20 million people lived in what is now Mexico. This number fell by 90 per cent over the next hundred years. Most of the original inhabitants were killed off by disease, war and slavery, brought in by the Spanish. Today, only a few Mexican Indians, including the Tarahumara and the Seri, live in the Mexican deserts. The famous Sioux and other native hunter-gatherer groups were wiped out by the Europeans, despite their fierce resistance.

▲ *This man is one of around 75 million Mexicans who are known as* mestizo *because of their mixed ancestry.*

◀ *This Mayan girl belongs to the small part of the population that is pure Mexican Indian. She speaks the Mayan language.*

Nevertheless, there were almost 10 million Mexican Indians in 2000. This included more than 1.3 million Nahua, descendants of the Aztecs, and 800,000 Mayas, who live in southern Mexico. In total, there are 56 distinct indigenous groups in Mexico and almost as many languages. Many still follow ancient religions and traditions. They farm maize and have respect for nature.

Ancient Mexican rituals have sometimes been mixed with Christianity. The Day of the Dead, for instance, is a festival which combines ancient culture with the Roman Catholic celebration of All Saints' Day.

▲ *A nun selling religious items in Mexico City. Seventy-nine per cent of the population are Roman Catholic.*

IN THEIR OWN WORDS

'My name is Maria Hernandes. I am 13 years old and I live in Oaxaca. We celebrate the Day of the Dead each year on 31st October. We come to the Jojotichlan graveyard, just outside the city. We sit down by the graves of the members of our family who have died and talk about them. It is not a sad occasion – everybody brings food and drink, and it's more like a party. People have been doing this for centuries and here in Oaxaca the festival is very famous.'

Population growth

The Mexican population has increased from 13.6 million in 1900 to an estimated 98.6 million in 2000. It is projected to grow to 133.8 million by 2025. Mexico had one of the fastest-growing populations in the world between 1970 and 1975. Then it was growing at a rate of 3.1 per cent each year. The rate has gone down drastically since then. It was 1.6 per cent each year between 1995 and 2000. People are better educated about birth control now. More women go to work and they often delay starting a family.

▼ *Approximately one-third of the Mexican population are children aged under 15.*

◄ *The Mexican birth rate has fallen in recent years. These young mothers are likely to have fewer children than their own mothers.*

IN THEIR OWN WORDS

'My name is Juan Carlos Hidalgo and I am 72 years old. I earn a little extra money by playing guitar. I play either on my own or in one of the *mariachi* bands that play at the weekend. I was born in a small village 60 km from the city of Zitácuaro. There were twelve of us in one little house and we all had to work in the fields. We grew mainly maize and kept a few pigs and chickens.

'At the end of the winter, there was often very little to eat, especially after a bad harvest. Three of my brothers and sisters died before I left home at 16. I don't earn much money today but at least I have enough so that my wife and I have food all year round. I also have three children who send money from time to time to help us in our old age.'

The Mexican population was very young during the 1970s and 1980s. A better balance between the age groups is gradually developing. Six per cent of the population were over 60 in 1997. This is expected to increase to 8.1 per cent by 2010. The increase in the elderly population shows that living standards have improved in Mexico.

Immigration

Many people emigrate to Mexico from other Central American countries. They are often trying to escape from war, poverty and human rights abuses. An estimated 40-60,000 people cross the border into Mexico from Guatemala every autumn. They come to harvest the coffee-bean crop and most of them return to Guatemala at the end of the season.

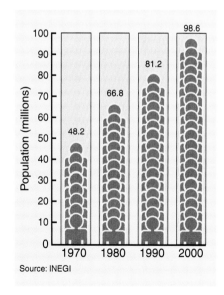

Source: INEGI

▲ *You can see how the Mexican population has grown over the years.*

THE CHANGING FACE OF MEXICO

Migration within Mexico

Over the last thirty years, approximately 10 million people have left the Mexican countryside. They head for the cities in search of work. By 1998, 80.2 per cent of the population were living in urban areas.

The most popular cities for migrants have been Mexico City, Guadalajara and Monterrey. The population of the Federal District of Mexico City increased from just over 3 million to almost 9 million between 1950 and 1980.

But more people have been moving north in the last ten years. This is because of the development of cities like Juárez and Tijuana. There are new work opportunities in tourism and the *maquiladora* industries (see pages 4 and 38). People who want to emigrate also come because the US border is so close.

Tijuana is in Baja California, where almost half the people are migrants. The city is popular with tourists, and with Mexicans on their way to the USA. Another favourite destination is Cancún. More and more tourists are coming to the city and thousands of jobs are being created. Cancún is in Quintana Roo, where over half the people are migrants.

Source: INEGI

▲ Look at the massive increase in the urban population over the last fifty years.

◄ The poverty of rural communities is worsening as people continue to leave for the cities in search of work.

Emigration to the USA

Approximately 150,000 Mexicans emigrate legally to the USA every year, and around the same number emigrate illegally. Most people go to the USA in search of better living standards. The 1990 US census showed that approximately 13.5 million Mexicans lived there.

▼ *The population of Mexico City has actually begun to fall as work opportunities increase in other parts of Mexico.*

IN THEIR OWN WORDS

'My name is Rosario Nochitlán. I am 17 years old and I live in Oaxaca City. My family moved here from our small farm, which was a six-hour bus journey away. We left behind our traditional lifestyle and now we all have different jobs in the city. I sell balloons in the main square, usually to the tourists. On fiestas, which are our country's religious holidays, Oaxacans bring their children to the square. Then they also buy from me.'

Changes at Home

Healthy living

Modern Mexico is seeing an improvement in its population's health. People are eating well and better health care is available. Because of these improvements, people are living longer.
The average Mexican was expected to live for 61 years in 1970. By 2000, the age had gone up to 75.3 years. This means that there will be many more elderly Mexicans in years to come. There are also fewer young babies dying. In 1970, approximately 69 out of every 1,000 babies died before they were one year old. By 2000, this had dropped to 25 deaths per 1,000.

▼ *Almost 90 per cent of infants are now vaccinated against measles, and 93 per cent against tuberculosis.*

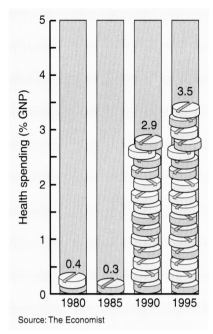

But these are averages for the whole country. There are still serious health problems for the people who live in Mexico's poorer states, like Guerrero, Oaxaca and Chiapas. Here, people die younger, and lose more of their children before they reach the age of one. They are also more likely to live in the traditional extended family and have a lot of children.

The country still has to bring a number of serious diseases under control. Nationwide vaccination programmes have been set up to fight disease and these are proving successful. Poliomyelitis, a crippling childhood disease, has been virtually wiped out, and there are far fewer cases of whooping cough and tuberculosis.

▶ *The government is putting a larger share of the country's money into health services.*

Source: The Economist

IN THEIR OWN WORDS

'My name is Juan Villa Real and I am 72 years old. I live in a small village about 20 km from the town of Quatrocienigas in the Chihuahua Desert. We are lucky enough to have fresh water and clean air. The soil is good and we grow maize, beans and walnuts.

'Most of the people here are healthy, which is just as well because there is only a small medical post at Quatrocienigas. The nearest hospital is in Torréon which is nearly three hours away by car. If someone needs to get help urgently, for instance, if they are bitten by a rattlesnake, they can't afford to wait around. I have my own pickup truck but a lot of people have to rely on the buses.'

Changing eating habits

The main food for most Mexicans is maize. It is usually eaten as a *tortilla*, which is a pancake made from maize flour. *Tacos*, which are rolled *tortillas* with meat, beans and spices, are a very popular meal. Mexicans also enjoy a vast selection of fruit, from apples and grapes in the north to coconuts and papayas in the south.

The diet of the rural population has not changed very much in recent times. However, people living in urban areas now have a wide range of foods to choose from. Most towns have hamburger restaurants and other fast food outlets.

The last 30 years have seen the average Mexican's diet improve. The amounts of calories, protein and fat people eat have all increased. It is usually considered unhealthy to eat more fat. But many Mexicans are so poorly fed that they actually need fat. A massive 40 per cent of the Mexican population is malnourished.

▼ *A taxi driver stops for a quick* taco. *Other traditional Mexican fast foods are* tortillas *and* empanadas *(meat pies).*

The government is tackling this problem in a number of ways. Subsidized milk and free school breakfasts are provided for over 4 million children. *Tortillas* are distributed to 1.6 million families. These measures are not nearly enough to cure the problem. The situation is most serious in rural areas.

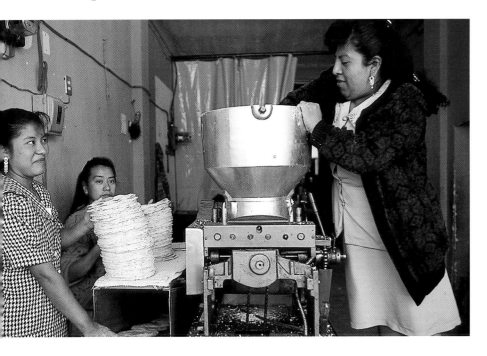

◀ *These women are using a special machine to make* tortillas *– the average Mexican eats 1 kg of* tortillas *every day.*

IN THEIR OWN WORDS

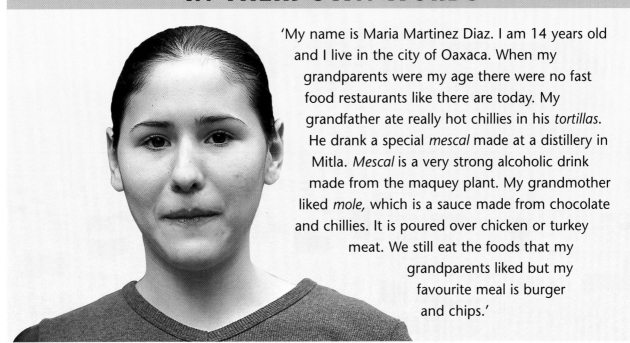

'My name is Maria Martinez Diaz. I am 14 years old and I live in the city of Oaxaca. When my grandparents were my age there were no fast food restaurants like there are today. My grandfather ate really hot chillies in his *tortillas*. He drank a special *mescal* made at a distillery in Mitla. *Mescal* is a very strong alcoholic drink made from the maquey plant. My grandmother liked *mole,* which is a sauce made from chocolate and chillies. It is poured over chicken or turkey meat. We still eat the foods that my grandparents liked but my favourite meal is burger and chips.'

Education

Improving the national education system is a priority for the Mexican government. It spends approximately 5 per cent of the Gross Domestic Product (GDP) on education. Primary education is free and compulsory for children aged between 5 and 11 years old. However, 40 per cent of primary school children still do not finish their schooling. If past trends continue that figure will increase.

◄ Rural schools suffer from lack of funds and overcrowding. This means that lessons often have to be held outside. A temporary cover has been set up for this class.

▼ In urban schools, even the younger children are getting access to modern technology.

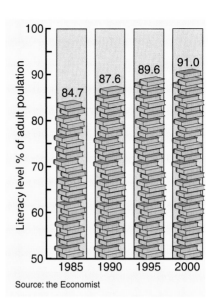

Secondary education was made compulsory for children aged between 11 and 14 in 1992. The government wanted to encourage pupils to stay on at school, so that they would go on to higher education. But most people cannot afford to carry on studying. In 1999, very few students, only 1.7 per cent of the population, were in higher education.

Urban schools usually have better facilities and smaller classes than those in the countryside. Average primary school class sizes fell from 39 to 28 between 1980 and 1998. Secondary school class sizes also fell, from 18 to 16. But rural schools often have much larger classes. This is because there are not enough schools and teachers in rural areas. Many remote areas have no secondary schools and children have to leave their villages to go to school. Some of the poorest families now get money from the government to send their children to school. There are also 4,800 training centres where young people are taught the skills they need to find work in industry.

▲ *The number of people with basic reading and writing skills is going up every year.*

IN THEIR OWN WORDS

'My name is Marie Carmen Jiménez. I am 11 years old and I live in Celestún. This is a picture of me with my younger sister Juanita. We go to the early school. We start at 7 am and finish at 12 noon. There are too many children in our school so half the children go in the morning and the other half go at 1 pm and finish at 6 pm.

'Next year I will go to the secondary school at the other end of town. There are too many children there too. Some of the classes are held outside on the sand. When I am 14 I will finish school and I don't think I will go to college. The nearest college is in Mérida, which is two and a half hours away on the bus and it costs a lot of money to get there.'

Leisure

Computer games and the Internet are increasingly popular with young Mexicans. Many towns now have Internet cafés where anyone can access the web for a small fee. Satellite TV has given many people in remote areas access to television for the first time.

Mexicans remain keen sports fans. Their favourites are football, basketball, baseball and volleyball. They also enjoy rodeos and the Mexican game of *Jai Alai*, which is played with a special glove and a small ball.

▼ *This house was too far away from the television transmitter to get any reception until the satellite dish was put up.*

◀ *Basketball is a favourite pastime for Mexican youngsters.*

Family life

It is usual for Mexican family members of different generations to all live together. Many families need the help of grandparents to care for the children while both parents are out at work. But modern living means that this family unit is often broken up. Many Mexicans have left their family homes in search of work. Even traditional family gatherings, such as the celebration of religious festivals, are becoming very difficult to organize.

Twenty years ago, the average family had six children. Women stayed at home to look after the family. But young women today expect to go out to work, marry later and have fewer children. By 1998, the average family had just 2.2 children.

The roles of husband and wife are also changing. Many families have to rely on both parents working to make enough money to survive. Couples often delay having children so that they can both work.

▲ *Many Mexicans still live in large extended families, like the Ramirez family pictured outside their home in Puebla.*

IN THEIR OWN WORDS

'My name is Teresa de Jesus Boteno Zunigo. I am 19 years old and I am studying to be a chemist at Monterrey University. Many things have changed for women since my mother was young. She was expected to stay at home and look after the children. I have decided to follow a profession. I chose chemistry because it is an area where there are possibly even more opportunities for women than men. When I qualify, I want to work for maybe ten years. I would like to marry and have a family, but first I want to work and have my own life.'

8 Changes at Work

In 1982 Mexico refused to pay the interest on the money it had borrowed from richer countries. As a result, loans for essential projects, such as road-building, were stopped. Mexico eventually had to start paying off its debts again. In order to do this, it had to change the way the country's business was organized. Mexico needed to raise money by selling goods to other countries. This meant that manufacturing industries became very important. More and more factories were built so that goods could be made for sale abroad. Mexico still has huge debts and has to pay off some US $12-13.5 billion in interest every year.

◀ *Another new factory is being built in Chihuahua. It will be used to make goods for sale to the USA.*

Export industries and the USA
In 1980 crude petroleum accounted for over 60 per cent of all Mexico's exports. The 1980s crisis brought about huge changes. Petroleum is now only 7.5 per cent of exports. By 1999 almost 90 per cent of exports were manufactured goods. This has influenced what is imported. Over 75 per cent of imports are for use in manufacturing.

◀ *This lorry is taking processed food to the USA. It has both US and Mexican number plates to make crossing the border quicker.*

Mexico's economy is heavily dependent upon its powerful neighbour, the USA. The USA received 90 per cent of Mexican exports in 1999. It is expected to remain Mexico's main trading partner well into the twenty-first century. Trade with Europe is easier since the new Free Trade Agreement was made with the European Union in March 2000. This may slightly reduce the importance of the US market for Mexico.

IN THEIR OWN WORDS

'My name is Jorge Alberto Martin. I am 18 and I live in the small town of Hunucmax about 30 km from the city of Mérida in the Yucatán. I am at college studying to become an engineer. Every weekday morning I leave home at 6 am. I take the bus to college in Mérida. I am hoping to work for our national oil company, PEMEX, in the state of Tabasco, where the main oil reserves are located. I think that I will have a good future working for an oil company. Mexico has huge reserves of oil, enough for another 50 years.'

Maquiladora industries

The traditional industrial cities of central Mexico have become less important over the last twenty years. This is because of the new *maquiladora* industries (see page 4). The northern cities of Chihuahua, Tijuana, Juárez and Monterrey now have successful *maquiladora* industries. They are close to the US border, which makes them well-placed to trade with the USA. In 1999 over half the industrial exports were from *maquiladora* factories. They raised a massive US $63.7 billion from sales to other countries. This was out of a total of US $99.7 billion brought in by all Mexico's exports in 1999. In the past four years alone, the growth has been dramatic.

◀ *The economy of Mexico City has benefited greatly from the growth of* maquiladora *industries.*

The number of *maquiladora* factories has increased from 3,047 employing 815,000 people in 1996 to 3,346 employing nearly 1.2 million in 2000.

Maquiladora exports to Europe are expected to increase following the new Trade Agreement. The city of Mérida, for instance, is ideally located for trade with Europe. It is expected to double its share of the total *maquiladora* export over the next five years.

This success is deepening the divide between rich and poor in Mexico. More money is now being made in the northern states and Mérida. Almost one-quarter of the country's money is still made by people in the area around Mexico City. But the poorest states, such as Oaxaca and Chiapas, still rely on small-scale farming. They have no immediate way out of grinding poverty.

▶ *This new shopping mall has been built on the outskirts of Mérida. It is a sign of the city's increasing wealth.*

IN THEIR OWN WORDS

'My name is Javier Jimínez Brito and I am 20 years old. I work as a taxi driver and I live with my wife Maria in Mérida. Maria works for a *maquiladora* company making expensive underclothes for a famous Italian fashion company. Once Mérida was a centre for the area's large farming economy. Now much of its wealth comes from the nearby oilfields in Tabasco. Mérida is the biggest and most important city in the Yucatán Peninsula. I am happy living in Mérida. I have my own car and I believe Mérida will carry on growing and there will continue to be plenty of work for me.'

Agriculture

Agriculture was once a main source of income for Mexico. It has been getting less and less important since the Second World War (1939–45). Even so, it still generates 5 per cent of the GDP and employs 23 per cent of the workforce. Coffee, sugar, fruit and vegetables are the main export crops. Maize, beans, wheat and sorghum are grown for sale within Mexico. Thirty per cent of Mexican agriculture is livestock, most of which is cattle and poultry.

Production of many major crops has been decreasing. This is largely due to how the land is owned. Half of Mexico's land belongs to the *ejido* system, in which land is held by a community. Until recently the community was not allowed to sell or rent out the *ejido*. As the land has been passed down through the generations, the plots have been repeatedly sub-divided. Millions of tiny farms have been created that make modern farming difficult. A law passed in 1992 allows people to apply for ownership of their land. By 2000 almost 3 million people had been given rights of possession, which can lead to ownership. Small plots are now being combined to form larger farms.

▼ *The alfalfa being grown in this field in the Chihuahua Desert is to be used as feed for dairy cattle.*

The fastest-growing and most productive farmlands are in the northern deserts of Chihuahua, Sonora and Sinaloa. Large irrigated farms grow everything from cotton to chilli peppers. However, these farms are over-exploiting underground water resources. This could result in reduced harvests in the future.

▶ *This market at Patzcuaro is full of fruit, vegetables and cereal crops like maize. They have been grown for sale in Mexio.*

IN THEIR OWN WORDS

'My name is Jorge Amando. I live in Delicias and I am an agricultural worker. The area around the Rio Conchos, close to Chihuahua City, is rich farming land. Only twenty years ago it was part of the Chihuahua Desert. Today the land is irrigated and we grow everything from cotton and chilli peppers to wheat and maize. We even keep large herds of cattle that produce milk for the city.

'Agriculture is the largest employer outside the city. Many more people are also employed in Chihuahua itself. They process agricultural products including milk, meat, cotton, chillies, potatoes and grapes.'

Service industries

Service industries include banking, computer-programming, tourism and catering, as well as public services such as rubbish collection. Almost 70 per cent of the money made in Mexico is made by service industries. They employ over one-third of the total workforce.

Tourism

Tourism is one of the most valuable of the service industries. It has shown steady growth for twenty years. Just under 6.2 million foreign visitors brought in a total of over US $4 billion in 1989. By 1999, over 10 million holidaymakers were bringing in US $5.4 billion. A further US $444 million income came from US day-trippers. The tourist industry employs 1.8 million people and the numbers are increasing as this area continues to grow. Ecotourism, when people come to see the beauty of the natural world, is increasingly popular. Visitors come to enjoy the spectacular reefs in the Gulf of Mexico, the monarch butterflies in Michoacán State and the whales off the coast of Baja California.

Women at work

Opportunities for women to work have increased as the population has become more urban. It is predicted that over half of all women will be employed by 2010. The *maquiladora* industries in the north need skilled workers and many women work in the factories. But women often have to take work on an informal basis. This means that they do not pay tax.

▼ *Playa del Carmen in the Gulf of Mexico is a favourite tourist destination.*

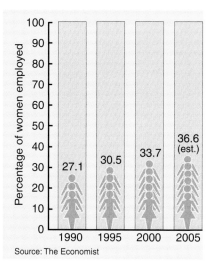

It also means that they have no rights. Women often work in low-paid agricultural and packing jobs. They have fewer opportunities for work than men and they receive lower wages.

◀ This Mayan woman is preparing dried sisal fibres. Sisal is used to make rope.

▲ The numbers of women at work are going up at a fast rate.

Source: The Economist

IN THEIR OWN WORDS

'My name is José Guerrera and I am 24 years old. I am a whale tour guide at Bahía de Magdalena, near La Paz, in Baja California. I first worked here as a helper with one of the tour companies. I managed to save enough money to buy a boat and set up my own company. Now I have four boats and all my brothers work with me.

'Every spring the whales come here and they attract more and more tourists from all over the world. If you had told me ten years ago that whales were valuable and that I could make a good living by taking people to see them, I would have laughed. Today I know a lot about the lives of whales, and I have a great house.'

The Way Ahead

At the beginning of the twenty-first century, Mexicans are hoping that the new government will give ordinary Mexicans a better quality of life. They also want an end to political corruption. President Vicente Fox has recognized that there are far too many of his people living in poverty. He was elected on promises to help the poorest in society. On average, Mexicans are better off today than thirty years ago. But in reality, the benefits are experienced by a few exceptionally rich people. Most Mexicans remain poor.

There is an extremely uneven distribution of wealth in modern Mexico. This is probably the most serious matter for the new President to deal with. Entire states are struggling against poverty, whilst others enjoy relative affluence. Successful Mexicans live in luxurious family homes in plush residential areas. But slum areas have also grown up in every major city. Mexico City has by far the worst problem. An incredible 30 per cent of its inhabitants live in *colonias populareo* (urban slums).

Nevertheless, the nation's health is constantly improving and the overall standard of living continues to go up. President Fox's party has taken over a thriving economy, which has been growing rapidly since 1995. The close connection with the USA means that Mexico's success relies on the continuing strength of the US economy.

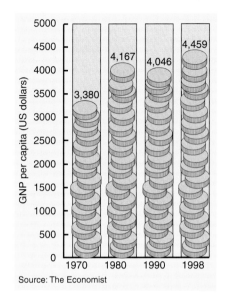

Source: The Economist

▲ *The average Mexican is much better off than thirty years ago.*

▼ *These cheap houses have been built in Chihuahua City because so many people are moving there. Many more houses like this are needed to solve the problem of city slums.*

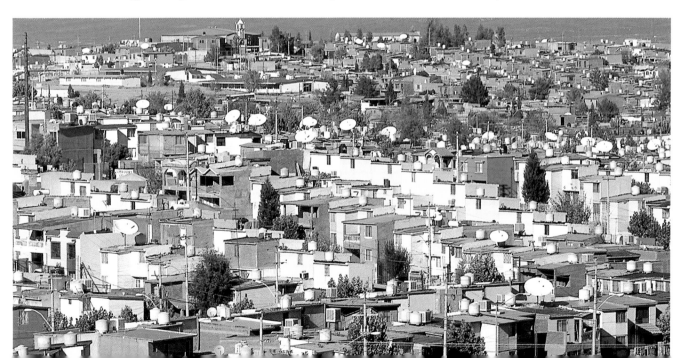

◀ *Better educational opportunities and management of natural resources are needed to safeguard the future for Mexico's children.*

IN THEIR OWN WORDS

'I am Juan José Reyna and I am 19 years old. I am a computer technology student at Monterrey University. I want to be a computer consultant. There are plenty of jobs in computers and I can make a lot of money in this profession. Once I am qualified I hope to work in other cities and perhaps I will even be able to get a job in the USA. But I plan to return to Monterrey after a few years. This is a beautiful city and I have a good future here.'

Glossary

Aztecs An ancient civilization at its peak when the Spanish invaded in 1519.

Chicle The sticky sap collected from chicle trees that is used to make chewing gum.

Deforestation The clearance of trees, either for timber or so that the land can be used for a different purpose.

Economy All the business activity in a country.

Ejido The Mexican word for communally-owned land.

Emigrate Go to live in another country.

Export Sell goods to another country.

Geothermal energy Energy produced by pumping water through the hot rocks in the Earth's crust.

Global warming The increase in temperature across the world thought to be due to pollution of the atmosphere.

Gross Domestic Product (GDP) The value of all the goods and services produced by a country, in that country.

Gross National Product (GNP) The value of all the goods and services produced by a country, including those produced abroad.

Hydroelectricity Electricity generated by water power.

Immigration Coming to live in a country from abroad.

Imported/imports Goods bought from another country.

Indigenous Belonging originally or naturally to a particular place.

Interest A charge for borrowing money, usually paid back as a percentage of what has been borrowed.

Irrigated Farmland supplied with water by a manmade system.

Malnourished Suffering from lack of nutrition due to a lack of food or a badly balanced diet.

Manufacturing Making goods.

Maquiladora An industry that is largely financed from abroad, where items are assembled in Mexico and sold elsewhere under recognizable brand-names.

Mariachi A traditional Mexican style of music.

Mayas Ancient civilization that flourished between 300 BC and AD 900.

Migration, migrants Moving to another area or country.

Peninsula A piece of land almost entirely surrounded by water or projecting far into a lake or sea.

Plantations Large estates where trees or plants are grown so that the timber or other produce, such as coffee, can be sold.

Plateau A high, flat area of land.

Quetzal A long-tailed bird: males are brightly coloured with green, red, blue and white feathers.

Rainforest Dense tropical forest with high rainfall.

Rights Those things due to a person if they are treated fairly.

Rural Countryside.

Sand bar A ridge of sand built up over time by the action of waves.

Sisal A stiff fibre used for making rope, from the Mexican plant of the same name.

Smelting Extracting metals from metal ores by heating.

Subsidized Partly paid for by the government.

Subsistence farming Producing only enough food for the farmer's own needs, rather than producing food to sell.

Temperate A milder, less humid climate than tropical.

Urban Built-up as in a town or city.

Further Information

Books

Insight Guide: Mexico, Insight Guides, 2000
Nations of the World: Mexico, Jen Green,
Raintree, 2003
World Art and Culture: Mexican, Elizabeth
Lewis, Heinemann Library, 2003
World Tour: Mexico, Sean Dolan, Raintree,
2003

Useful addresses

Friends of the Earth,
26-28 Underwood Street,
London N1 7JQ
Tel. 020 7490 1555
Website: www.foe.co.uk

The Hispanic and Luso Brazilian Council,
Canning House, 2 Belgrave Square,
London SW1X 8PJ
Tel. 020 7235 2303 ext. 221/2
Website: www.canninghouse.com

Latin America Bureau,
1 Amwell Street,
London EC1R 1UL
Tel. 020 7278 2829
Website: www.lab.org.uk

Oxfam GB,
274 Banbury Road, Oxford OX2 7DX
Tel. 0870 333 2700
Website: www.oxfam.org.uk/coolplanet/

Save the Children Fund,
17 Grove Lane,
London SE5 8RD
Website: www.savethechildren.org.uk

Survival
6 Charterhouse Buildings
London EC1M 7ET
Tel: 020 7687 8700
Website: www.survival-international.org

World Wide Fund For Nature (WWF),
Panda House, Weyside Park,
Godalming, Surrey GU7 1XR
Tel. 01483 426444
Website: www.panda.org

WWF in Mexico
Website: www.wwf.org.mx

Websites for statistics on Mexico

Institute Nacional de Estadística Geografíae
Informática (INEGI) at www.inegi.gob.mx

United Nations Development Programme
(UNDP) at www.undp.org

United Nations Children's Fund (UNICEF) at
www.unicef.org

The website addresses (URLs) included in this
book were valid at the time of going to press.
However, because of the nature of the
Internet, it is possible that some addresses
may have changed, or sites may have
changed or closed down since publication.
While the authors and Publishers regret any
inconvenience this may cause the readers,
no responsibility for any such changes can
be accepted by either the author or the
Publisher.

Index